INCLINED PLANES
AND WEDGES

by Sally M. Walker and Roseann Feldmann
photographs by Andy King

Lerner Publications Company • Minneapolis

For my son, Tim, love you forever —RF

*The publisher wishes to thank the Minneapolis Kids program
for its help in the preparation of this book.*

*Additional photographs are reproduced with permission from: © Owen Franken/Corbis, p. 10;
Marathon Letourneau Company, p. 12; © Paul A. Souders/Corbis, p. 13; © David J. Sams/
Stone, p. 24; © Layne Kennedy/Corbis, p. 26; © Steve Callahan/Visuals Unlimited, p. 30;
© Bob Rowan/Progressive Image/Corbis, pp. 31, 47; © RDF/Visuals Unlimited, p. 35; © D.
Yeske/ Visuals Unlimited, p. 43.*

Text copyright © 2002 by Sally M. Walker and Roseann Feldmann
Photographs copyright © 2002 by Andy King

Lerner Publications Company
A division of Lerner Publishing Group
241 First Avenue North
Minneapolis, MN 55401 U.S.A.

Website address: www.lernerbooks.com

Library of Congress Cataloging-in-Publication Data

Walker, Sally M.
  Inclined planes and wedges / by Sally M. Walker and Roseann Feldmann;
photographs by Andy King.
     p.   cm. — (Early bird physics books)
  ISBN 0-8225-2221-7 (lib. bdg. : alk. paper)
  1. Inclined planes—Juvenile literature. 2. Wedges—Juvenile literature. [1. Inclined
planes. 2. Wedges.] I. Feldmann, Roseann. II. King, Andy, ill. III. Title. IV. Series.
TJ147.W35 2002
621.8'11dc—21   00-010578

Manufactured in the United States of America
2 3 4 5 6 7 – JR – 07 06 05 04 03 02

CONTENTS

BE A WORD DETECTIVE

Can you find these words as you read about inclined planes and wedges? Be a detective and try to figure out what they mean. You can turn to the glossary on page 46 for help.

complicated machines
force
friction
gravity

inclined plane
simple machines
wedge
work

You do work when you plant flowers. What are other examples of doing work?

Chapter 1

WORK

You work every day. At home, one of your chores may be planting flowers. At school, you work when you climb the stairs.

You are working when you climb up a ladder. You work when you eat your breakfast. It may surprise you to learn that playing and eating are work, too!

You do work when you play.

When scientists use the word "work," they don't mean the opposite of play. Work is using force to move an object from one place to another. Force is a push or a pull. You use force to do chores, to play, and to eat.

You use force when you cut paper.

This girl is moving a box from one place to another, so she is doing work.

Sometimes you push or pull an object to move it to a new place. Then you have done work. The distance that the object moves may be long or short. But the object must move.

Pulling a sled uphill is work. Your force
moves the sled to the top of the hill.

You use force when you pull your sled up a hill.
You are doing work.

These children are using force to push against this tree. But the tree is not moving. Are the children doing work?

Pushing a very large tree is not work. It's not work even if you sweat. It's not work even if you push until your arms feel like rubber. No matter how hard you try, you have not done work. The tree has not moved. If the tree falls over, then you have worked!

A bulldozer is a machine with many moving parts. What do we call machines with many moving parts?

Chapter 2

MACHINES

Most people want to make doing work easier. Machines are tools that make work easier. Some of them make work go faster, too.

Some machines have many moving parts. We call them complicated machines. It may be hard to understand how complicated machines work. Escalators and bulldozers are complicated machines.

An escalator is a complicated machine.

A staircase is a simple machine.

Some machines are easy to understand. They are called simple machines. Simple machines have few moving parts.

Simple machines are found in every home, school, and playground. They are so simple that most people don't realize they are machines.

A doorknob has few moving parts.

It is a simple machine.

This girl is using an inclined plane. What kind of machine is an inclined plane?

Chapter 3

INCLINED PLANES

An inclined plane is a simple machine. An inclined plane is a flat surface. One end is higher than the other. Using an inclined plane makes it easier to lift or lower heavy objects.

16

You can prove this for yourself. You'll need four or five thick books, a heavy weight, and the board from a family game. The heavy weight might be a 5-pound bag of flour. Or you could use a very large can of food.

You can show that an inclined plane makes work easier. These are the things you will need.

Stack the books on a table. Put the weight next to the books. Try to lift the weight up onto the books with one hand. Use two hands if you have to. Lift it several times. Lifting the weight straight up takes a lot of force.

 It takes a lot of force to lift a heavy object by yourself.

Next, lean the game board against the books. The game board should be folded in half. The top end of the board should be near the edge of the top book. You have turned the board into an inclined plane.

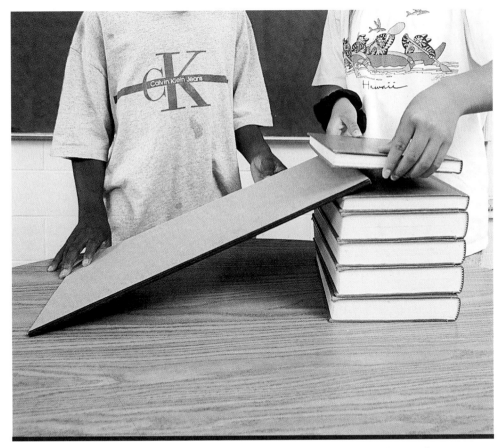

Place another book on the high edge of the game board.
The book will help keep the board in place.

Slide the weight up the inclined plane.
You can probably do this with just one hand.
Pushing the weight up the inclined plane is
easier than lifting it. Pushing takes less force
than lifting the weight straight up.

An inclined plane makes it easier to move a
heavy object to a higher place.

This girl is lifting a picnic basket to the top of a fort. The basket is heavy, so she must use a lot of force. How much force is she using to lift the basket?

Here the basket is hanging from a spring scale. A spring scale measures force. This spring scale is measuring how much force the girl is using to lift the basket.

This girl is using about 17 units of force to lift the basket.

Here the girl is using about 7 units of force.

This time the girl tries something new. She uses the slide as an inclined plane. She puts the basket on the bottom of the slide. Then she pulls it up the slide. The spring scale shows that the girl is using less force. Pulling the basket up the slide is easier than lifting it.

The girl pulled the basket a longer distance. But her work was easier. She used less force.

This person is climbing a ladder. The ladder is the shortest distance from a low place to a high place. But the climber must use a lot of force to get to the top.

A straight ladder is the shortest distance from a low place to a high place. But a climber must use a lot of force.

A staircase is easier to climb than a ladder. You travel a longer distance on a staircase. But you use less force.

A staircase is an inclined plane. Climbing a staircase is easier than climbing up a ladder. The climber travels a longer distance. But climbing each step takes less force. The inclined plane makes it easier for the climber to get to a higher place.

This man is using an inclined plane to move a heavy block of ice. How is the inclined plane helping him?

Chapter 4

GRAVITY AND FRICTION

An inclined plane makes it easier to move an object from a high place to a low place. You can prove it.

Put the heavy weight up onto the pile of books. Lower it back down to the table. Lower the weight several times. Lowering the weight back to the table takes a lot of force.

It takes a lot of force to lower a heavy object.

Next, push the weight up the board. When the weight is near the top, let go. What happens?

Push your weight to the top of your inclined plane.

An inclined plane makes it easy to lower a heavy object.
Gravity pulls an object down an inclined plane.

The weight slides back down the inclined plane. You don't have to push it. The inclined plane made it easy to lower the weight back to the table. Why was it so easy?

Gravity made it easy to lower the weight. Gravity is a force that pulls objects toward the ground. Gravity is the force that pulled the weight down the inclined plane.

Gravity pulls a sled down a snowy hill.

A hill is an inclined plane. A snow-covered hill is great for sledding. Gravity pulls the sled down the hill. But another force acts on the sled, too. The other force is called friction. Friction is a force that stops or slows moving objects.

There isn't much friction between a sled and the snow on a hill. So the sled slides easily down the hill.

There isn't much friction between two smooth surfaces. A surface is the outside of an object. Icy, packed snow and the bottom of a sled are both smooth. There isn't much friction between them. So a sled slides easily on packed snow. There would be a lot of friction between a sled and grass. The friction between them would stop the sled from moving. That's why people don't sled on grassy hills.

There isn't much friction between the weight and the game board. The weight slides easily.

Put the heavy weight on the top end of the game board and let go. The weight slides fast because the board is smooth. There isn't much friction between the board and the weight. The smooth board helps the weight slide quickly, the same way snow helps a sled slide.

How could you change the amount of friction on your inclined plane? Put a bath towel on the game board. Try sliding the weight down. How fast does it slide?

A towel will change the amount of friction on your inclined plane.

The weight probably didn't slide at all. Or maybe it slid very slowly. The surface of a towel is bumpy. There is a lot of friction between the towel's bumpy surface and the weight. There is enough friction to slow or stop the weight, the same way grass would stop a sled.

Friction can stop a heavy object from sliding down an inclined plane.

This man is using a ramp to move a heavy object.

A ramp is an inclined plane. Some ramps are smooth. Their slippery surface does not have much friction. It is easy to slide a weight up or down a smooth ramp. It is much easier than moving a weight straight up or down.

An inclined plane makes doing work easier. Traveling a longer distance lets a person use less force. A person can use even less force going down an inclined plane because gravity helps.

You can make another simple machine with two inclined planes. What kind of simple machine can you make?

Chapter 5

WEDGES

Look at some doorstops in your school. Some of them are inclined planes. You can make another simple machine if you put two of those doorstops together. You can make a simple machine called a wedge. A wedge is two inclined planes put together.

A wedge's pointed end makes it easier to move things apart. Try pushing the flat end of your wedge into the dirt. Then try pushing the pointed end into the dirt. It's much easier. That's why the tip of a shovel is shaped like a wedge.

Two inclined planes together make a wedge.

Using a wedge makes work easier. You can prove this. You will need a nail, two thick books, and the plastic lid from a tub of margarine. Ask an adult to help you.

A wedge makes doing work easier. You can prove this for yourself.

Push the point of the nail through the lid. Be careful not to stick your finger. The pointed wedge on the end of the nail moves the plastic apart. The wedge makes it easier to push the nail into the lid.

Place the lid on top of two books, like this. Then you won't stick yourself when you push the nail through the lid.

Slide the lid along the body of the nail. It may be hard to do. There is friction between the body of the nail and the lid. The friction makes it harder to slide the lid along the nail.

 *Why is it hard to slide the lid along the nail?*

It would take a lot of force to push a flat object through a lid. It takes much less force to push a wedge through a lid.

Pull the nail out. Try pushing the flat head of the nail through the lid. Can you do it? You probably can't. Pushing the flat end of the nail through the lid would be very hard work. The wedge at the tip of the nail makes the work much easier.

A nail easily pushes wood apart. Wedges can push apart many materials.

The tip of a nail is a wedge. It is easy to hammer the tip of a nail into wood. Why? It is easy because the wedge pushes the wood apart.

What force stops the nail from sliding out? There is friction between the body of the nail and the wood. Friction helps to hold the nail tightly in place.

Using simple machines gives you an advantage. An advantage is a better chance of finishing your work. Using an inclined plane or a wedge is almost like having a helper. And that's a real advantage.

 Using a simple machine is almost like having a helper.

ON SHARING A BOOK

When you share a book with a child, you show that reading is important. To get the most out of the experience, read in a comfortable, quiet place. Turn off the television and limit other distractions, such as telephone calls. Be prepared to start slowly. Take turns reading parts of this book. Stop occasionally and discuss what you're reading. Talk about the photographs. If the child begins to lose interest, stop reading. When you pick up the book again, revisit the parts you have already read.

Be a Vocabulary Detective

The word list on page 5 contains words that are important in understanding the topic of this book. Be word detectives and search for the words as you read the book together. Talk about what the words mean and how they are used in the sentence. Do any of these words have more than one meaning? You will find the words defined in a glossary on page 46.

What about Questions?

Use questions to make sure the child understands the information in this book. Here are some suggestions:

> What did this paragraph tell us? What does this picture show? What do you think we'll learn about next? What does it mean to do work? Is pushing against a tree work? Why/Why not? What is a simple machine? How do simple machines make work easier? What are some examples of inclined planes and wedges? Can you find these simple machines in your classroom or home? What is your favorite part of the book? Why?

If the child has questions, don't hesitate to respond with questions of your own, such as: What do *you* think? Why? What is it that you don't know? If the child can't remember certain facts, turn to the index.

Introducing the Index

The index helps readers find information without searching through the whole book. Turn to the index on page 47. Choose an entry such as *friction* and ask the child to use the index to find out how friction can slow down or stop a moving object on an inclined plane. Repeat with as many entries as you like. Ask the child to point out the differences between an index and a glossary. (The index helps readers find information, while the glossary tells readers what words mean.)

SIMPLE MACHINES

Books

Baker, Wendy, and Andrew Haslam. *Machines*. New York: Two-Can Publishing Ltd., 1993. This book offers many fun educational activities that explore simple machines.

Burnie, David. *Machines: How They Work*. New York: Dorling Kindersley, 1994. Beginning with descriptions of simple machines, Burnie explores complicated machines and how they work.

Hodge, Deborah. *Simple Machines*. Toronto: Kids Can Press Ltd., 1998. This collection of experiments shows readers how to build their own simple machines using household items.

Van Cleave, Janice. *Janice Van Cleave's Machines: Mind-boggling Experiments You Can Turn into Science Fair Projects*. New York: John Wiley & Sons, Inc.: 1993. Van Cleave encourages readers to use experiments to explore how simple machines make doing work easier.

Ward, Alan. *Machines at Work*. New York: Franklin Watts, 1993. This book describes simple machines and introduces the concept of compound machines. Many helpful experiments are included.

Websites

Brainpop—Simple Machines
<http://www.brainpop.com/tech/simplemachines/> This site has visually appealing pages for levers and inclined planes. Each page features a movie, cartoons, a quiz, history, and activities.

Simple Machines
<http://sln.fi.edu/qa97/spotlight3/spotlight3.html> With brief information about all six simple machines, this site provides helpful links related to each and features experiments for some of them.

Simple Machines—Basic Quiz
<http://www.quia.com/tq/101964.html> This challenging interactive quiz allows budding physicists to test their knowledge of work and simple machines.

GLOSSARY

complicated machines: machines that have many moving parts. Bulldozers and escalators are complicated machines.

force: a push or a pull. You use force to do chores, to play, and to eat.

friction: a force that stops or slows moving objects

gravity: the force that pulls objects toward the ground

inclined plane: a flat surface with one end higher than the other. Ramps and staircases are inclined planes.

simple machines: machines that have few moving parts. Inclined planes and wedges are simple machines.

wedge: two inclined planes put together. Nails and shovels are wedges.

work: using force to move an object from one place to another

INDEX

About the Authors

Sally M. Walker is the author of many books for young readers. When she isn't busy writing and doing research for books, Ms. Walker works as a children's literature consultant. She has taught children's literature at Northern Illinois University and has given presentations at many reading conferences. She lives in Illinois with her husband and two children.

Roseann Feldmann earned her B.A. degree in biology, chemistry, and education at the College of St. Francis and her M.S. in education from Northern Illinois University. As an educator, she has been a classroom teacher, college instructor, curriculum author, and administrator. She currently lives on six tree-filled acres in Illinois with her husband and two children.

About the Photographer

Freelance photographer Andy King lives in St. Paul, Minnesota, with his wife and daughter. Andy has done editorial photography, including several works for Lerner Publishing Group. Andy has also done commercial photography. In his free time, he plays basketball, rides his mountain bike, and takes pictures of his daughter.

METRIC CONVERSIONS

WHEN YOU KNOW:	MULTIPLY BY:	TO FIND:
miles	1.609	kilometers
feet	0.3048	meters
inches	2.54	centimeters
gallons	3.787	liters
tons	0.907	metric tons
pounds	0.454	kilograms